ZOOM!

Life on Earth

First published in this edition in 2004 by Cherrytree Books,
a division of Evans Brothers Ltd, 2A Portman Mansions,
Chiltern St, London W1U 6NR

Copyright © 2002 Orpheus Books Ltd.

Created and produced by Nicholas Harris and
Claire Aston, Orpheus Books Ltd.

Text Nicholas Harris

Consultant Steve Parker, Scientific Fellow of the
Zoological Society

Illustrated by Inklink, Firenze

Other illustrators Gary Hincks

ISBN 1 842342 29 0

A CIP record for this book is available from the British
Library.

Printed and bound in Singapore.

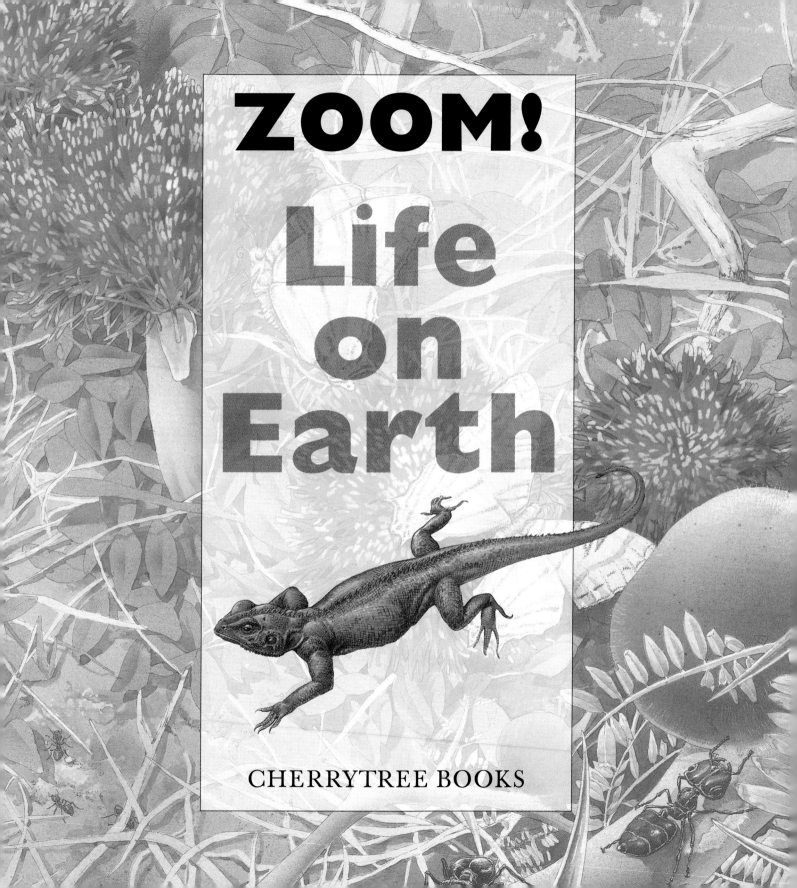

ZOOM!

Life on Earth

CHERRYTREE BOOKS

LET'S ZOOM!

When you use the zoom feature on a camera, you bring pictures from distance to close-up without moving it. For example, you can capture the image of a butterfly on a leaf while keeping your distance. This book works in exactly the same way.

Imagine you were able to travel into space and point a camera back at the whole Earth. The illustration on pages 6 and 7 shows what you would see in your viewfinder. Now zoom in to one part of Earth's surface—the spectacular East African Rift Valley. You'll find yourself looking at a landscape of ancient volcanic calderas, set amid grassy plains peppered with trees and bushes. Keep zooming, and you will begin to see some of the amazing inhabitants of this wild savannah landscape: elephants, giraffes, zebras, lions and many of the other famous safari animals. Zoom in further and many much smaller and less familiar creatures of the undergrowth come into view. You'll discover the flowers hidden away in that undergrowth, ants creeping up a flower stalk and—zooming into a new microscopic world—bacteria that live on an ant's body.

It's a fascinating journey, yet you will not have to move one millimetre! And you will discover some amazing things about life on Earth that only this incredible *zooming* book can show you …

Sahara Desert

Arabia

AFRICA

Great Rift Valley

EARTH

Our planet is one of nine planets in the Solar System. It is the only known world to have life, thanks to the presence of liquid water and to its atmosphere, which shields Earth both from the Sun's harmful rays and from bombardment by large, rocky objects from space.

Earth is sometimes compared to a giant spaceship. It travels through space (at more than 100,000 kilometres per hour) and everything that lives on it must depend on its own resources for survival. Essentials, such as water and nutrients, are recycled in nature, for the benefit of all Earth's living things *(see pages 23 and 26)*.

ASIA

INDIAN

OCEAN

ZOOM DOWN TO AFRICA, ONE OF EARTH'S SEVEN CONTINENTS

7

RIFT VALLEY

We are in East Africa, looking down at the Great Rift Valley, a huge, spectacular geological feature created by the pulling apart of tectonic plates *(see page 22)*.

Upwelling magma from deep beneath Earth's crust fills the gap left by the separating plates. The crust stretches, thins and eventually rifts along a series of cracks, called faults. A long, narrow block

LOOK FOR THE GREAT RIFT VALLEY IN EAST AFRICA

of land sinks between the faults to form a rift valley. In East Africa, this valley runs all the way from Mozambique in the south to the Red Sea in the north.

With magma not far from the surface, volcanoes old and new pepper the Great Rift Valley. Calderas, huge craters left behind after volcanoes explode, are also common. Some act as natural shelters for wildlife that live on the savannah grasslands within their walls.

TAKE A CLOSER LOOK INSIDE A CALDERA

SAVANNAH

Savannah *(see page 25)* covers this part of the Great Rift Valley. Although dominated by grasses, there are also many bushes and trees, including acacia, baobab and whistling thorn. The climate is hot and dry from June to October, with a rainy season running from November to May.

Grazing herds of animals move around according to where they can find grass and water. When the dry season begins, they migrate from their breeding grounds in the south to wetter areas in the north.

Here in the wide caldera, the water-hole is a focus for much of the local wildlife. Tracks leading to it from every direction reveal the paths they regularly take. Vultures circle overhead, scanning the ground for dead or dying animals.

ZOOM DOWN TO THE WATERHOLE TO SEE THE ANIMALS

Lion

Marabou stork

ANIMALS

The savannah grasslands of East Africa are home to a wide range of plant-eating animals. The grazers—those animals that feed on grass—include zebras, which eat the coarse tops, and gazelles, which crop the shoots close to the ground. Among the leaf-eaters are giraffes, which eat from the topmost shoots of the trees, and elephants which take leaves (and bark) from lower down. Rhinoceroses feed on small shrubs and plants.

Giraffe

LOOK FOR THE ANIMALS ROAMING ACROSS THE SAVANNAH

The savannah's meat-eating animals prey on some of the plant-eaters. The lion catches its victims by making short bursts from the cover of long grass or bushes. Scavengers, including storks, vultures and hyenas (which also make their own kills) feed on the carcasses left behind by lions and others.

Rhinoceros

Zebra

Hippopotamus

Elephant

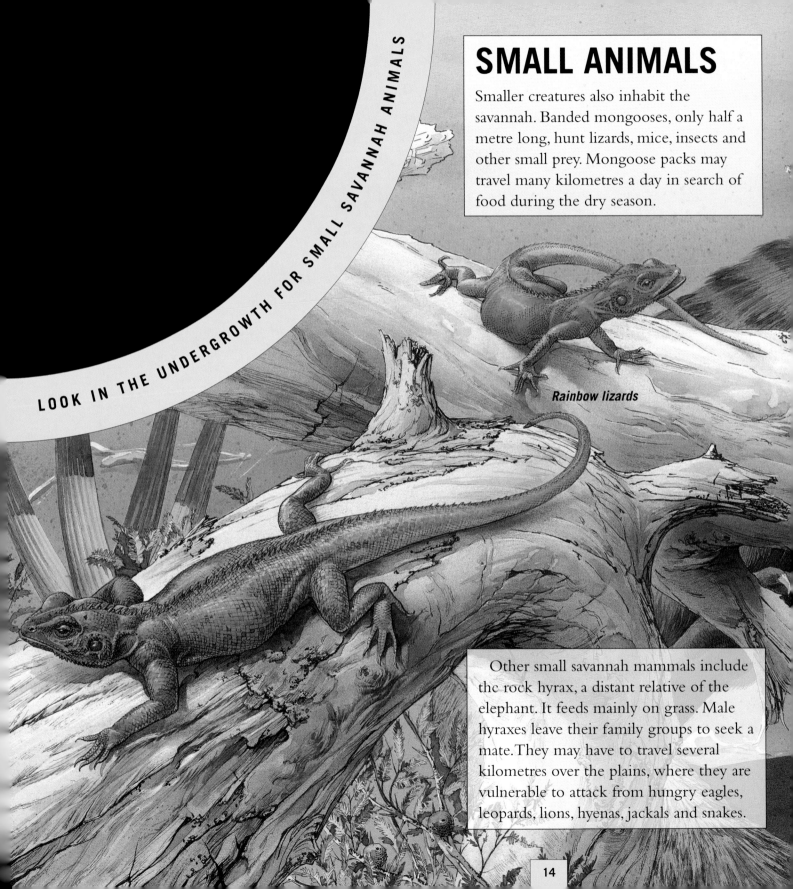

SMALL ANIMALS

Smaller creatures also inhabit the savannah. Banded mongooses, only half a metre long, hunt lizards, mice, insects and other small prey. Mongoose packs may travel many kilometres a day in search of food during the dry season.

Rainbow lizards

Other small savannah mammals include the rock hyrax, a distant relative of the elephant. It feeds mainly on grass. Male hyraxes leave their family groups to seek a mate. They may have to travel several kilometres over the plains, where they are vulnerable to attack from hungry eagles, leopards, lions, hyenas, jackals and snakes.

Banded
mongoose

Rock hyrax

ZOOM IN CLOSE TO THE FLOWERS AND HERBS

SOME SMALLER ANIMALS FEED ON PLANTS AND INSECTS

FLOWERS AND HERBS

Growing among the savannah grasses are certain other flowers and herbs that are exactly suited to a climate where it is dry for half the year. They grow well in the rich soil, made fertile by the weathering of volcanic rock *(see page 23)* found everywhere in the Great Rift Valley.

The colourful flower petals, strong scent and presence of a sugary liquid called nectar all attract butterflies and bees to the plants. As they feed, they pick up sticky pollen grains which brush off at the next flower they visit, so enabling the plants to reproduce.

ANTS

Insects are very important members of the savannah community *(see page 27).* Some kinds, such as locusts, swarm together and eat huge amounts of vegetation. Butterflies and bees help spread pollen, allowing plants to reproduce. Other insects play their part in decomposing dead plants and animals and recycling nutrients for other living things to take up. Termites carry dead plant matter into their nests, where they grow fungus on it to eat. Dung beetles remove animal waste and use it both for food and for laying their eggs in.

Common among the insect life of the savannah are ants. They are social insects: they live in large groups, known as "colonies", within which each individual plays a part to benefit the rest.

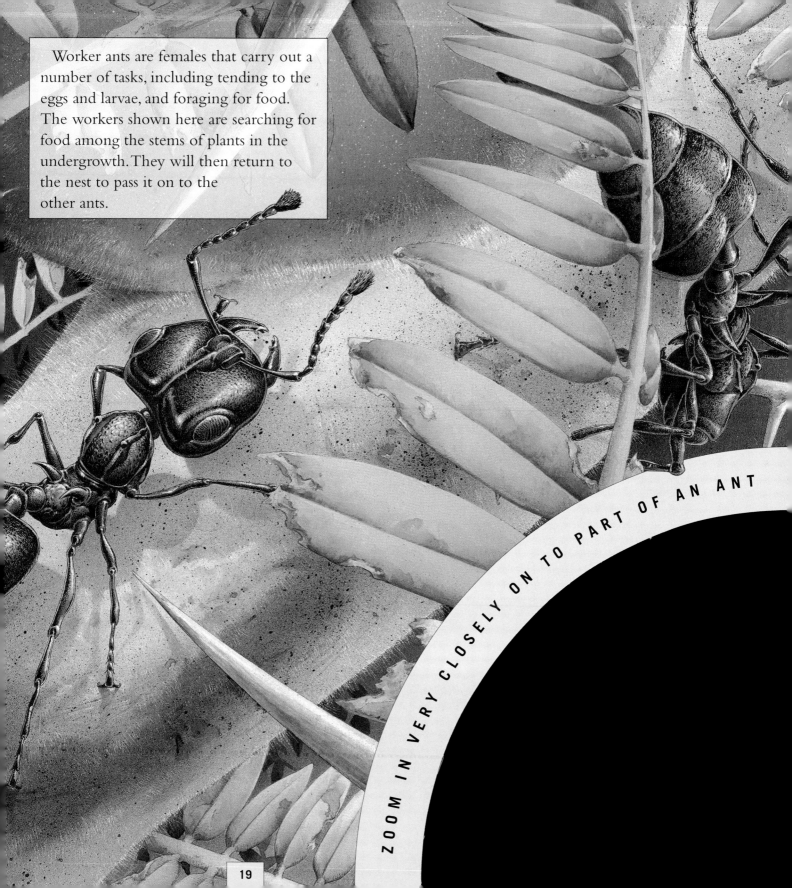

Worker ants are females that carry out a number of tasks, including tending to the eggs and larvae, and foraging for food. The workers shown here are searching for food among the stems of plants in the undergrowth. They will then return to the nest to pass it on to the other ants.

ZOOM IN VERY CLOSELY ON TO PART OF AN ANT

BACTERIA ARE FOUND EVERYWHERE IN THEIR BILLIONS

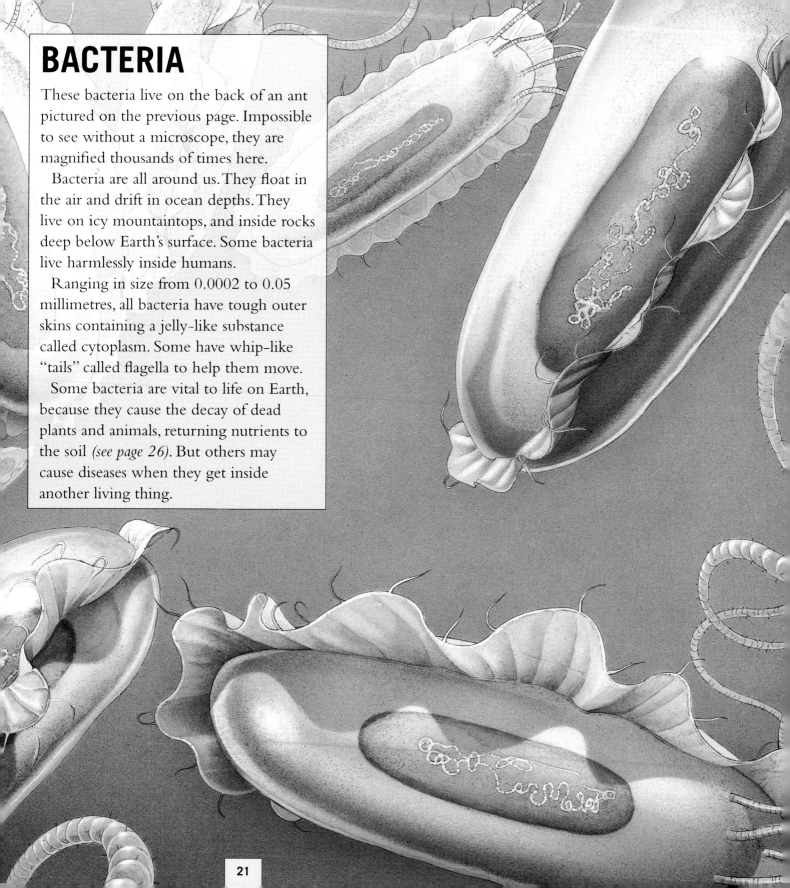

BACTERIA

These bacteria live on the back of an ant pictured on the previous page. Impossible to see without a microscope, they are magnified thousands of times here.

Bacteria are all around us. They float in the air and drift in ocean depths. They live on icy mountaintops, and inside rocks deep below Earth's surface. Some bacteria live harmlessly inside humans.

Ranging in size from 0.0002 to 0.05 millimetres, all bacteria have tough outer skins containing a jelly-like substance called cytoplasm. Some have whip-like "tails" called flagella to help them move.

Some bacteria are vital to life on Earth, because they cause the decay of dead plants and animals, returning nutrients to the soil *(see page 26)*. But others may cause diseases when they get inside another living thing.

PLANET EARTH

Earth is made up of several layers *(right)*. The outer layer is a thin rocky **crust** just a few tens of kilometres thick. Beneath it lies the **mantle**, divided into the upper mantle, consisting of a mix of molten and solid rock, and the lower mantle, a band of rock made solid by the pressure of the layers above. At the centre lies the **core**, made mostly of iron. The outer core is liquid, while the inner core is solid. The temperature rises from 1500°C at the base of the crust to 7500°C at the centre of Earth.

Earth's outer shell is divided into about 15 jagged-edged pieces, called **tectonic plates**. In some places the edges collide and crumple up to form mountains. In others, the plates are pushed apart by magma (molten rock) rising from the mantle. Plates slide beneath others around the edges of some oceans *(below)*, often triggering volcanic eruptions and earthquakes. Plates sliding past one another in the opposite direction (as along the San Andreas Fault in California) also cause earthquakes.

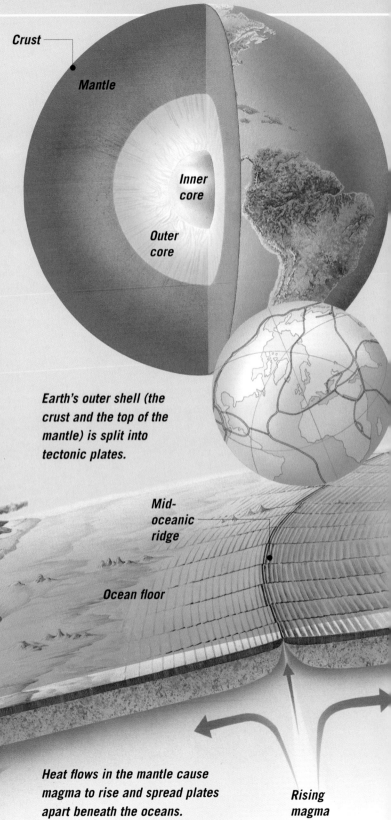

Crust

Mantle

Inner core

Outer core

Earth's outer shell (the crust and the top of the mantle) is split into tectonic plates.

Volcano

Ocean trench

Mid-oceanic ridge

Ocean floor

Plate sliding down

Continent

Heat flows in the mantle cause magma to rise and spread plates apart beneath the oceans.

Rising magma

Earth is the only planet to have liquid water. It circulates between its surface and the atmosphere, the blanket of air that surrounds the planet, in an endless cycle known as the **water cycle** *(right)*.

The water cycle plays a vital role in shaping Earth's surface. Hard and permanent as they seem, all rocks are vulnerable to **weathering**. Sharp changes in temperature crack open rocks. Rainwater seeping into rock crevices expands as it freezes, splitting off pieces. Constant battering by waves and rivers or slow grinding by glaciers wear away the rocks. Over millions of years, wide valleys and eventually the levelling of mountain ranges result from this process of **erosion**.

Sedimentary rocks, such as sandstone and limestone, are made from sand, gravel, mud and the other fragments that result from erosion (or from the remains of living things). As layers build up, they

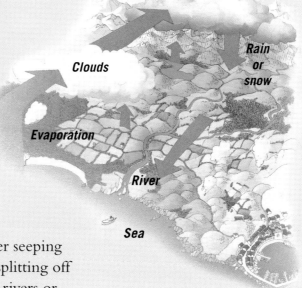

Warmed by the sun, water evaporates from lakes, rivers and the oceans. The moisture is carried upwards where it cools and condenses (turns back into liquid water). Tiny water droplets or ice crystals gather around dust particles to form clouds. Eventually they fall as rain or snow. Rivers carry the water back to the ocean.

are compressed into rock. **Igneous rocks**, such as granite and basalt, are formed when magma rises, cools and solidifies in the Earth's crust. **Metamorphic rocks**, such as marble and slate, are formed when rocks are subjected to great pressure and heat. The three different types change from one to another in the **rock cycle** *(below)*.

Sedimentary rocks formed under the sea may sink into Earth where one tectonic plate slides under another (opposite). They may then melt, rise and cool to become igneous rocks. Sedimentary rocks may also be crushed or cooked under the ground to form metamorphic rocks. All types of rock may be eroded, becoming sedimentary rocks again. This continual process is known as the rock cycle (right).

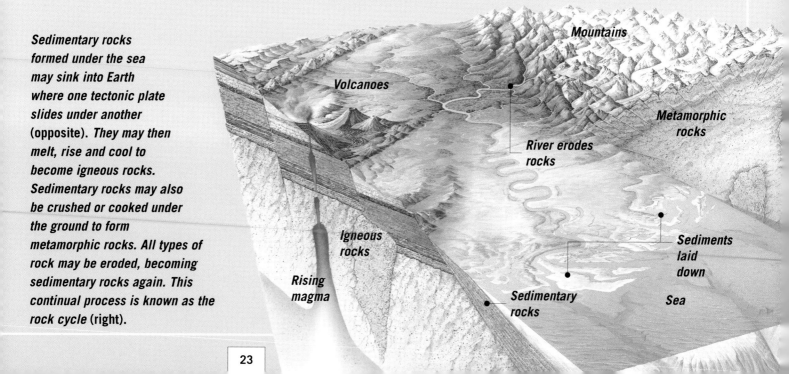

23

CLIMATES AND BIOMES

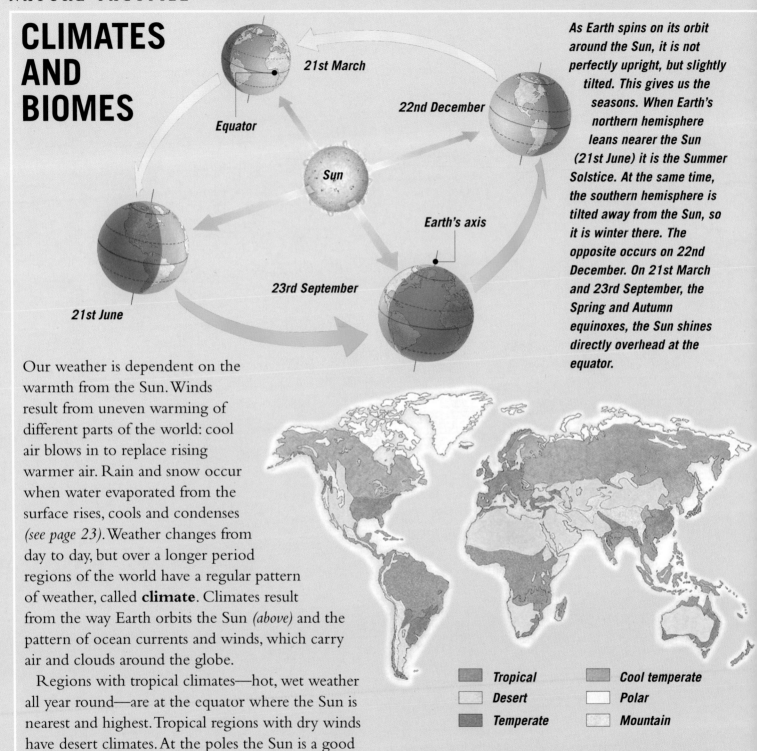

21st March

Equator

Sun

22nd December

Earth's axis

23rd September

21st June

As Earth spins on its orbit around the Sun, it is not perfectly upright, but slightly tilted. This gives us the seasons. When Earth's northern hemisphere leans nearer the Sun (21st June) it is the Summer Solstice. At the same time, the southern hemisphere is tilted away from the Sun, so it is winter there. The opposite occurs on 22nd December. On 21st March and 23rd September, the Spring and Autumn equinoxes, the Sun shines directly overhead at the equator.

Our weather is dependent on the warmth from the Sun. Winds result from uneven warming of different parts of the world: cool air blows in to replace rising warmer air. Rain and snow occur when water evaporated from the surface rises, cools and condenses *(see page 23)*. Weather changes from day to day, but over a longer period regions of the world have a regular pattern of weather, called **climate**. Climates result from the way Earth orbits the Sun *(above)* and the pattern of ocean currents and winds, which carry air and clouds around the globe.

Regions with tropical climates—hot, wet weather all year round—are at the equator where the Sun is nearest and highest. Tropical regions with dry winds have desert climates. At the poles the Sun is a good deal lower in the sky, so it is much colder. Between the tropics and the poles are temperate lands which have warm summers and cool winters.

▉ Tropical	▉ Cool temperate
▢ Desert	▢ Polar
▉ Temperate	▢ Mountain

The pattern of world climates is partly influenced by ocean currents. For example, northwestern Europe is warmed by the flow of the Gulf Stream from the tropics.

A **biome** includes all areas where the vegetation and animal life are broadly similar. Biomes are shaped by climate (and also the local rocks and soil type). Each biome consists of a range of **habitats**. A temperate woodland biome, for example, may be made up of oak, beech or maple habitats.

Earth's polar regions (1) are mostly covered by snow and ice. Close to northern polar lands is the tundra (2), a region too cold for trees, but where the snow melts in summer to let mosses grow.

Boreal coniferous forest (3) covers much of northern Russia and North America, while deciduous woodland (4) grows in warmer climates.

Most deserts (5) are bare and rocky. A few are sandy. Savannah grasslands (6) are hot and dry but also have a rainy season *(see page 10)*. Tropical rainforest (7) has high rainfall all year round. It is home to the richest variety of living things. The largest biome is the ocean (8). Most ocean life lives on or near the sea bed in shallow waters.

NATURAL CYCLES

The plants and animals of any habitat require **nutrients**—minerals and other substances—for maintenance and growth. In nature, chemical elements, such as oxygen, carbon and sulphur, that make up nutrients are recycled via plants and the soil *(below)*. In this way they are always available.

Plants take up nutrients in the soil through their roots (1). They use them, along with carbon dioxide from the air and light energy from the Sun, for nourishment. Plant-eating animals digest the nutrients in their food (2). The nutrients may pass on to a meat-eating animal, or return to the soil when either animal dies (3). Meanwhile, carbon dioxide breathed out by animals returns to the air. Fungi, microbes and soil animals all help the rotting process by which living things decay and release the nutrients, to be taken up by plants once more (4).

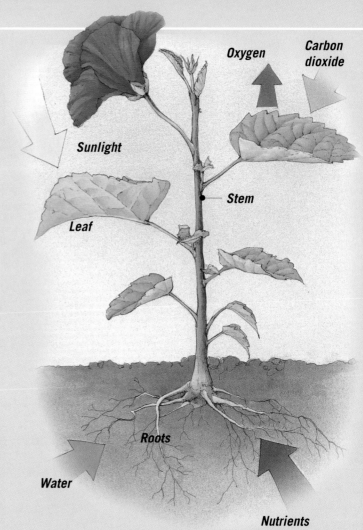

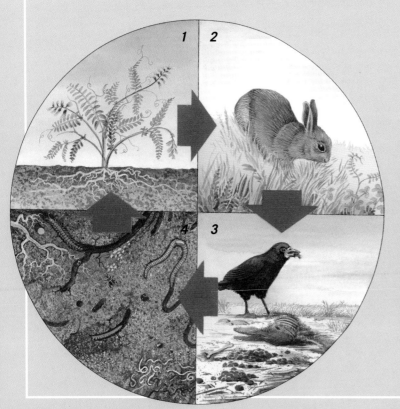

Plants play a vital role in the recycling of both nutrients and oxygen *(above)*. A plant's roots are the means for taking in nutrients and water from the soil. Its stem holds it above the surface and supports the leaves. Its leaves are "food factories". A green substance called chlorophyll absorbs the energy in sunlight which the plant uses to make a chemical reaction. Water from the soil and carbon dioxide from the air join together to form sugar, the plant's food. This process is called **photosynthesis**.

In this chemical reaction, plants also produce oxygen, which seeps out into the air and is breathed in by animals.

Living things in any habitat interact and rely on each other for survival. Together, they form a **community**. Plants "feed" on sunlight, water and nutrients from the soil on land, or from the water around them in the ocean. Animals, in turn feed on plants. Known as **herbivores**, they range from tiny insects to mammals and birds. Animals that eat animals are called **carnivores**. The linking of plants and animals in this way is called a **food chain**. In nature, animals eat more than one kind of food— for example, a bear may eat herbivores, insect-eaters and insects themselves—so food chains are part of more complicated **food webs**, such as this one *(right)* from a North American forest. If one animal or plant in a food chain disappears for any reason, it can have disastrous effects on the food web.

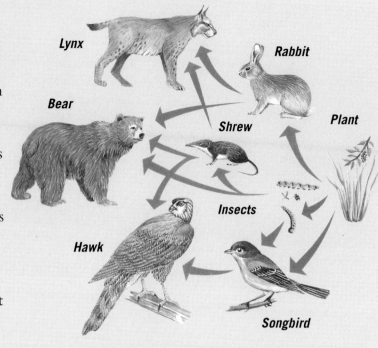

Lynx
Rabbit
Bear
Shrew
Plant
Insects
Hawk
Songbird

The moneran kingdom includes bacteria. Each is a single microscopic cell without a nucleus (control centre). Protists are single-celled organisms that have nuclei.

An individual living thing in a community is called an **organism**. To understand how organisms live, it helps to classify them or put them into groups, known as kingdoms: monerans, the smallest, simplest organisms, protists, slightly more complex organisms, fungi, plants and animals *(see page 28)*.

Fungi obtain their energy directly from dead and dying organisms, by causing them to decompose then absorbing the nutrients. Plants receive their energy from sunlight, while animals live by feeding on other living things. The animal kingdom includes many different kinds of invertebrates (animals without backbones) such as arthropods, molluscs, worms, sponges and jellyfish.

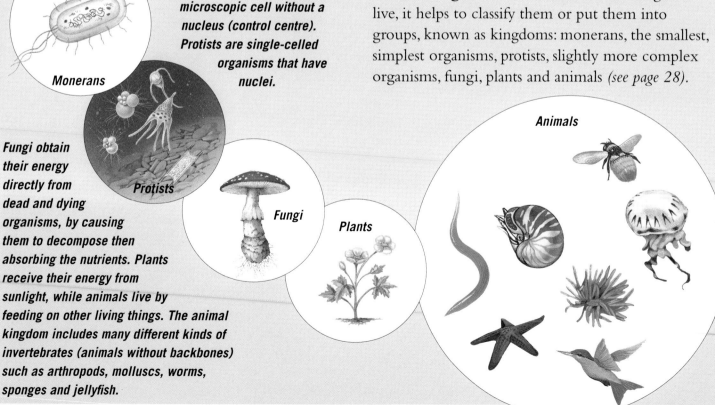

Monerans
Protists
Fungi
Plants
Animals

27

ANIMAL GROUPS

Swallowtail butterfly

Toad

Invertebrates: (animals without backbones): this group includes many marine creatures (sponges, jellyfish, sea anemones, molluscs and crustaceans), microorganisms (protozoa), insects, spiders, millipedes and centipedes.

Amphibians: animals that return to water to breed. They include newts, salamanders, frogs and toads. The young are aquatic and breathe using gills. Adults develop lungs.

Great white shark

Manta ray

Seahorse

Salmon

King cobra

Fish: aquatic (water-living) animals that breathe by means of gills. They are cold-blooded, hairless and streamlined in shape. Many have a protective layer of overlapping scales. Their fins help them to balance and steer.

There are two main groups: cartilaginous fish (skeletons made of soft cartilage: sharks, rays and chimaeras) and bony fish (skeletons made of bone: e.g. seahorses, salmon, cod, eels etc.)

Reptiles: cold-blooded, mainly land-living animals with scaly skins. They include lizards, snakes, turtles and crocodiles. Most reptiles lay eggs. Reptiles need to bask in the sun to raise their body temperature before they can move about.

Green turtle

Birds: warm-blooded, feathered animals with front limbs adapted into wings for flight.

Ostrich

Mammals: warm-blooded animals that give birth to live young. They then feed them with milk. The monotremes (platypus and spiny anteater) lay eggs. Except for whales and dolphins, all mammals have four limbs and a covering of hair or fur.

Kangaroo

Among the flightless birds are the ostrich, emu, kiwi and all penguins.

Marsupials are mammals that do not give birth to fully developed young. The young are born at an early stage, then develop in their mother's pouch. Marsupials include kangaroos, koalas, and possums.

Noctule bat

Chipmunk

Mammals have adapted to all a wide range of habitats, such as oceans, polar regions, and mountains The bats can fly.

Falcon

Red fox

There are about 9000 species of bird. They include seabirds, waterfowl, birds of prey, storks, swifts, kingfishers, cuckoos and many types of perching bird.

Mammals range in size from tiny rodents to giant whales. Some mammals graze or eat leaves, while others are flesh-eaters.

Asian elephant

Bird of paradise

Humpback whale

GLOSSARY

Arthropods Animals with hard external skeletons and pairs of jointed legs. They include insects, crustaceans, spiders and millipedes.

Atmosphere The envelope of gases that surrounds a planet, moon or star.

Bacteria Tiny organisms made up of only one one cell. Some live inside other organisms. Some types cause disease. Bacteria play a vital role in recycling nutrients in the soil.

Biome A large group of habitats that are generally similar to one another.

Caldera A round basin formed after a violent volcanic eruption during which the volcano collapses in upon itself.

Cell A tiny "building block" which makes up all the tissues in all living things.

Climate The pattern of weather in a particular region of the world over a long period of time.

Crust The thin, rocky outer layer of the Earth.

Food chain The sequence in which a plant is eaten by an animal, which is then eaten by another animal, and so on. Because animals eat more than one kind of food, food chains are part of more complex food webs.

Fungi Living things, such as mushrooms, that feed on rotting plant and animal material and reproduce by shedding spores.

Habitat The type of surroundings in which a plant or animal lives.

Invertebrates Animals without backbones.

Magma Hot melted, or molten, rock, that is formed beneath the Earth's crust.

Mantle The layer of the Earth that lies beneath the crust and the core, its innermost portion.

Migration The movement of a population of animals from one place to another at a certain time of year to feed or breed.

Moneran An organism that is made up of a single cell without a nucleus. Bacteria are monerans.

Nutrients Substances needed to maintain an organism's bodily activity and new growth.

Organism Any living thing

Photosynthesis The process by which plants use sunlight as an energy source to turn carbon dioxide and water into the sugars they need for food.

Pollen Microscopic grains that are produced in the male part of a flower and transferred to the female part of another (or the same) flower during pollination.

Protist An organism that is made up of a single cell containing a nucleus.

Rift valley A valley formed by the sinking of land between parallel faults.

Savannah Tropical grasslands with scattered trees and bushes.

Tectonic plates The large slabs into which Earth's surface is divided. The plates move relative to one another.

Weathering The action of rain, wind, heat or frost on decaying or disintegrating rocks.

Vertebrates Animals with backbones.

INDEX